Digital Marketing for Small Businesses

How to Market your Products and Services Online

Asim Akram

www.StarWebMarketing.com

Why Digital Marketing?

By implementing digital marketing strategies and tactics you will get more leads, customers, and sales compared to conventional marketing strategies and tactics, PERIOD.

Dedication

To my wife for supporting me through all ups and downs and standing by me even when I was not at my best.

Introduction

So you've just started your business. Exciting, isn't it?

Gone are the days when you need to have a huge marketing budget to launch your brand. With the internet changing the business landscape as we know it, small businesses now have a fighting chance at taking on even the big national brands. Even local businesses have a chance at worldwide fame — all thanks to online marketing.

While some business owners may look at digital marketing as optional back when the internet was still in its early days, it has actually become a necessity for survival in these modern times. When people hear about a new business, usually the first instinct is to look up the website or check out the social media accounts. If they can't find information about this new business online, they question its legitimacy, or worse, they doubt its existence. Consumer behavior has changed drastically over the past years and, as a business owner, you have no other choice but to keep up.

If you want to discover the secrets that will grow your small business using online marketing techniques, this book will teach you everything you need to know. From creating a digital marketing strategy for your business, to establishing your presence on most online marketing avenues, you'll learn techniques that will help you increase your brand's visibility, attract leads, and turn them into sales.

This is your first step to reaching hundreds of thousands of potential customers online. Don't miss out on this unique opportunity to take your small business to the big leagues.

The hardest challenge is to start. Are you ready for it?

TABLE OF CONTENTS

Chapter 1: Creating your Online Marketing Strategy 1

Chapter 2: Creating your Company or Product Website 13

Chapter 3: Content Marketing 21

Chapter 4: Social Media Marketing 39

Chapter 5: Social Media Platforms 49

Chapter 6: SEO and SEM 61

Chapter 7: Google Analytics 67

Chapter 8: A/B Testing 73

Chapter 9: Email Marketing 75

Chapter 10: Funnels 83

Chapter 11: Marketing Challenges and Solutions 87

Conclusion 94

CHAPTER 1

Creating your Online Marketing Strategy

According to recent statistics, around half of the world's population already has access to the internet. With around 3.2 billion people going online every day, connecting with people from all over the world has become a lot easier. We now live at a time when information, any form of information, is just a click away, and we always want more and at a quicker pace—we could safely say that the internet is a place that is constantly evolving to reach higher plateaus.

Even if you run a local small business, having some form of online presence is absolutely crucial in this day and age; most people, especially young men and women, look through the internet before checking any other source for every single kind of information. Therefore, your local business having a presence on the internet is paramount because existing and potential customers expect to see you online. These days, it has become common for people to check the internet first to get information about a brand or a company. Even with a storefront that you've been running for years, you will seem more credible if you have a website, or at the very least, an active Facebook page, so it's not surprising to see digital marketing taking the center stage when running a brand on the internet.

> *It's not surprising to see digital marketing taking the center stage when running a brand on the internet.*

Taking your business online may seem overwhelming, but with the right online marketing strategy, you can see your brand grow to its full potential. Here are the basic steps to build your online marketing strategy.

Clarify your brand message

The first thing that you need to think about is your brand. You may have a business name, a logo, even a website, but if you don't stand for something, you can't claim to have a brand. This is why you need to ask this question: what is it that you want your business to be known for?

Your brand differentiates you from all the other businesses that are just like you. Your brand connects your business to the market that you want to reach. And if you back it up with excellent products and exceptional customer service, your brand keeps making the clients come back to you, which means maintaining a high income.

Clarifying your brand message is actually very simple. You just need to take the time to think about the direction you want your business to go. Think of why you started the business in the first place. Look at the progress you've already made at this point and reflect on the accomplishments that you feel proud of the most. Evaluate how you run your business and see what practices or values set you apart from your competition. Once you've gone through all these questions, your brand and brand message should be much clearer to you. Here are some pointers that might be of good use for you, which we are going to develop as we continue:

1. Have one big goal and several small ones. Goals are a great way to understand where you want to head as a brand; it simplifies a lot of different aspects of your business and it allows everyone involved to understand what the main target is. Therefore, it is highly recommended to establish the brand's main goal and several little targets that might be achieved over the short, medium, and long term. You may want to be able to get a certain level of interaction on Facebook after two months. You may want to get a certain weekly traffic to your website after one month. These are all small targets that shape the way your brand and your working team are going to operate in the foreseeable future.

2. Develop a tone for your content. A brand message is not only what you say and what you aspire to be, but also the way the message is delivered. That is very important to take into consideration; the tone can shape the way your content is going to be received and the reactions it may produce. Be serious, be funny, be witty, be lighthearted, be anything that you want to be, but always with honesty and consistency so that people can be convinced of what they are hearing and reading.

3. Don't make things too complicated. A message can transmit ideas, intentions, emotions, and a lot more, but it has to do it through a certain lens of simplicity; you are not going to get people's attention through a very intricate and complex message because the results are going to be discouraging, to say the least. This is why you have to work hard on what you want to transmit and how to transmit it, to get far better results and a much more positive reception from your target audience. Speaking of which...

Know your target audience

A target audience is the people you are directing your content to and who might be the best fit for the type of area in which you are working. You need to know the people you're serving, or the people who are most likely to pay you money for the products or services that you're offering. You may think that you will be more successful by targeting anyone and everyone, but that would be an impractical move because you are never going to have the budget to reach everybody and content designed to appeal to everyone is going to come out as impersonal and lackluster. Even the most successful companies had the smarts to target a specific demographic in the population because they understand that going after a vague target market will only result in scattered efforts.

Knowing the people who will be part of your audience will put you in a better position to deliver better products and services to them because you're focused on meeting their needs. Sure, it may seem like you're shutting your doors on a segment of the population that doesn't fit your criteria, but here's another way to look at it: by focusing your efforts, you'll be more efficient and effective in reaching out to people who are likely to buy from you. This just means better and bigger business in the long run.

So how do you know who your target audience is? By figuring out the demographic that needs your products and services the most. You can start with the basics like age, gender, location, income level, occupation, education level, family, or marital status.

Once you have that down, you can move on to the psychographics like attitudes, personality, values, hobbies and interests, lifestyles, and buying behavior. Doing research on your target audience may seem like tedious work, but once you've created your buyer personas, it will be simpler for you to craft brand messaging and marketing strategies that will resonate with them.

You'll often hear business experts say that it's cheaper to retain an already existing client than to try to win a new one. But what exactly does this mean and how is it relevant to your online marketing strategy? While attracting new clients can feel rewarding, it involves hours of hard work and expenses. Before you can convince someone to choose you over the competition, you need to put in the time conceptualizing and executing campaign ideas. You'll also need to spend money on some paid ads so that they'll pay attention to you. You'll probably give a discount on their first purchase just to move them along to the buying stage.

Attracting existing clients on the other hand, is much easier and cheaper with a higher chance of converting their interest into repeat sales. If they've had a good experience with you in the past, all you need to do is send them a promotional email about a sale coming up, and they'll be there, ready to buy.

So don't just focus on strategies to attract new clients to your business. You should also think of ways to keep the clients you already have. Think retention programs like loyalty discounts and birthday freebies so that you give them more reasons to keep on coming back to you. Some of the following advice might be of good use to you:

1. Cycles of renewal are heathy and necessary. While it is true that you have to keep your regular audience happy and satisfied with the content and services that you are providing, it is also very important to keep things fresh and to keep yourself updated with what is going on in your field–that is when the cycles of renewal come to the scene. Maybe every three to six months you could have a look at the strategies you have been using and do a few tweaks, changes, and updates to secure much better results.

2. Listen to your audience's opinions and reactions. You are not going to be a successful brand without a faithful following and that is a key element to take into consideration. People's reactions, opinions and thoughts can come a long way for your brand to stand above the rest of your competition; the reality is that there are a lot of companies and businesses that do not pay much attention to their following, which results in half-successful outputs, so you have to separate yourself from that particular area and provide much more complete services and content.

3. Do cycles of questionnaires and polls. Yes, cycles once again. Another way of getting your target audience's opinions and thoughts is through questionnaires and polls about your brand, what you offer, how you offer it, and many other elements. This is simple and to the point, thus making sure that you are going to get the information that you require on several aspects and allowing your target audience to have the kind of involvement that they definitely want with your brand, if they are interested in it.

Target audiences can make or break a brand, so it is very important that you define this from the get-go because time that you waste focusing your content on a kind of audience that is simply not interested is time that you could focus somewhere else.

Clearly define your business goals

We promised that we were going to focus a lot more on certain areas and here we are! Once you have a clearer understanding of your brand and your target market, you can then start defining your business goals. To define your business goals, try to picture where you want your business to be one year, or five years, or even ten years from now. What kind of operations do you want to have by then? How much revenue do you want to be earning? What are the things you need to do to turn your vision into reality?

***Time that you waste focusing your content on a kind of audience that is simply not interested is time that you could focus somewhere else.**

Your business goals are basically what you expect your company to accomplish within a timeframe. Business goals not only serve as a guide for the team to ensure that everyone's on the same page, it's also the most coherent way to measure the success of your business.

So how do you define your business goals? You define it the **SMART** way. What is the **SMART** way? Let's have a look right here:

- o **S**pecific - Answer all the W questions (who, what, where, when, why, which) to clearly define your goals. The more specific you are, the better your chances will be of actually achieving your goals. Clarity is paramount to establish a goal.

- o **M**easurable - You should be able to measure the progress of all the goals you set. Set concrete mile markers to help you stay on track of every goal you set. For example, instead of a vague "increase sales" goal, opt for something like "increase conversion rate by 2%" or "increase unique visitors by 1,000." Numbers matter and this is something that plays a big role within any kind of company and the digital marketing element of the equation is no different, of course.

- **A**chievable - Do you have the capacity or the potential to actually achieve your goals? Remember, having a solid plan is crucial in achieving your goals, which is why we already explained that you should have a big goal and small ones to accomplish in the short, medium, and long term.

- **R**ealistic - Somewhat related to achievable, your business goals should also be realistic. There should be a good balance between how much you're willing to work and how able you are to work towards your goals. You have to remember that Rome was not built in a day and the same goes for your brand– take the time to make every single step in the best possible way and that way you will grow at a somewhat slow, but steady pace.

- **T**ime Specific - Setting goals within a specific time frame gives you a sense of urgency to achieve them. Without a time frame, you'll only end up procrastinating. Sure, the time frame has to be realistic and adjustable to your resources, so that is something worth taking into consideration.

Targets are a very important element because they are going to help you to develop a certain direction and focus, which is one of the most important things to do when you are merely starting out in the business of digital marketing, especially if you are handling a small business.

Set your KPIs

As we previously stated, numbers play a big role when managing a brand in every single aspect; it is the way in which we keep track of the increase or decrease in results, so it is paramount that you start to develop automatisms about how to use these elements to your advantage and obtain better results.

In this regard, Key Performance Indicators, most commonly known as KPIs, help you track and measure where you are in achieving your goals. Many online marketers use KPIs to prove that their efforts have a positive impact on their overall goals and to have a certain level of consciousness of where they are at the moment, thus providing much better strategies in the short, medium, and long term. Since measuring success of an online marketing campaign may seem like a complicated process, you need to set which specific KPIs to measure. Buyer conversion is one of the most common KPIs that marketers measure because at the end of the day, all your marketing efforts should result to more sales.

Here's how to set your online marketing KPIs:

- o Check if your KPIs align with your business goals. There's no point to setting KPIs that aren't connected to what you want your business to achieve.

- o Make sure that your KPIs are measurable and quantifiable. **"Increasing profit"** is a bit vague compared to "increasing revenue by 50% over the next six months."

- Choose the right metrics that will help you measure your success. If one of your KPIs is to earn $300,000 in a month, then one of your metrics that will determine if you're successful is how much you should earn per day. You can consider yourself a success if you earn $10,000 daily.

- Once you've set your KPIs, use them to check on your progress on a regular basis. Don't forget to set alerts for days when you don't reach your KPI. Make sure to keep everyone in the loop and share your KPIs with the team. Having KPIs is an effective way to see if your online marketing strategy is producing the results that you're aiming for.

Consistency and detail are two essential characteristics for any kind of success, so it is not surprising that this is something that we should all apply when it comes to digital marketing; KPIs are a pretty good answer to that and they provide the kind of tracking and insight that we all require to get a much better output from our strategies.

CHAPTER 2

Creating your Company or Product Website

With most business transactions happening online, it's important for any small business to have their own company or product website. Even if the products or services you have on offer are not being sold directly over the internet, a website can increase your credibility and visibility to potential clients. A professionally designed website can make clients feel more confident to do business with you because they feel that they know you a bit more, just by visiting your website.

And we have to be completely blunt in this particular aspect: if you don't have a website, your brand may lose a bit of credibility. Why? Because nowadays having a website for any brand is a standard that has to be maintained in order to get much better results and that is why when someone Googles your brand and doesn't find a website, he or she tends to lose interest and that is something you should never forget.

But what makes good company websites truly great? And what kind of skills do you need to get your own company website up on the internet? We are about to provide those answers for you.

If you want to create a great company website, you need to make sure that it speaks clearly to your audience. Your website should provide your potential clients with all the information they're looking for, no matter what stage they are at in the buying process. It's a plus if it's nice to look at, but more than that, you need to think of it as a primary tool that will help you reach your business goals.

Building your first company website may seem overwhelming, especially for those who are practically clueless about designing a website. Don't worry; it's actually more doable than most people make it out to be. Here you are going to find everything you need to know about building and launching your very own business website.

Your website should provide your potential clients with all the information they're looking for, no matter what stage they are at in the buying process.

Align your website and business goals

Since each business serves a different purpose, you need to set specific goals for your website that are aligned to your business goals. For example, if your goal is to sell your products online, then you need to create an ecommerce website that is conducive for online shopping. If your goal is to inform clients about how the service you're offering can make their lives better, then you need to have a blog on your website. Is your goal to develop tech products that customers can rely on? Then your site needs to have access to 24/7 tech support.

You can start this by doing research on websites of brands that might be of a similar ilk to you or may provide similar characteristics. This is a great way to learn from others who have already done it and take what works for your brand and discard what doesn't–that way everything is going to work the best for you.

Create your site structure

Once you've set clear goals for the website, the next step is to create a site structure. Having a defined structure will help you create your website's content plan so you don't end up with a random collection of different pages and blog entries that serve no clear purpose on your website. A site structure makes your website usable, and at the same time, discoverable by your target audience. Planning the content on your website at this stage will also help you develop an effective SEO strategy later on.

Choose your domain and host

A domain is like your own piece of real estate on the internet. Having your very own .com is one of the easiest ways to increase your business' credibility online. While there are some platforms that offer free domains that come with extensions, yourbrand.com sounds more professional than yourbrand.someoneelsesbrand.com. Plus, it's easier to remember. After you've decided on a domain, the next step is to choose a reliable hosting platform. If you're on a budget, shared hosting is a great option for beginners as they're usually very simple to use.

Pick out a theme

Themes will give your website its unique artistic appeal so make sure to pick out a theme that fits your branding perfectly. Your theme should represent what your brand stands for so if your catch phrase is somewhere on the lines of simple and modern, hold off on the frilly embellishments.

Also, not many small business owners will have the resources to get a design team to work on their theme, so one practical way is to check out pre-made themes that are available online for a small fee. While there are many free themes that you can choose from, they are often not as secure as those that you need to pay for. Some tips that might be of good use for you are the following:

- Always maintain the same tone in the writing part. As we previously stated; the website needs to have the same style that your target audience is going to have on your social media platforms in order to have a certain consistency.

- Make sure that the website is aesthetically pleasing; presentation comes a long way to make a positive impression on your target audience to make sure that they feel welcomed and comfortable in this particular ambiance.

- Combination of colors is also helpful. It has been scientifically proven that certain combinations of colors can be far more appealing to the general public, thus contributing to customers feeling much more attracted to your website and what you have to offer.

Tell your brand story the best way you can

One of the best ways to connect with your audience is through your website so make sure to tell your brand story the best way you can. Share how you started the business from the beginning, what your values are, and the journey you've taken to reach your goals. People respond better to businesses with a story to tell so find creative ways to tell them more about your small business. Experiment with different types of content on your website and see which ones get the most engagement from your audience. Some tips that we can provide for you are:

- o Be engaging. Have fun writing this story and this will transmit to your target audience; enthusiasm is palpable and cannot be ignored when people are intrigued by what you have to say.

- o Keep it simple. While a few details here and there are the key elements to a great story in any format, it is very advisable that you keep things simple, so people can understand it without much issue.

- o Highlight the highlights. Yes, it may sound weird on paper, but all we are trying to say is that you should point out what your brand's greatest achievements are so far in order for your target audience to see that you are a capable and well-suited brand for what they may need.

Use the right photos

Visuals have the power to take your content to a whole new level so make sure to use the right photos for your website. Aside from product photos, try including team photos, as well as high-quality stock images to add visual appeal to your business website. Just remember to steer clear of cheap stock photos, especially if it doesn't add any value to the content you have. Sometimes you're better off with no photo instead of resorting to low quality images. And don't exaggerate with the amount of pictures; unless your brand has something to do with photos and/or imagery, it's better if you just have a few images here and there as a complement of sorts.

Add a contact form

Your website isn't just a platform for your business to reach out to your audience; it can also be a means for your audience to connect with you and that can make a big difference in terms of questions, doubts, and many other issues that might be troubling them. Aside from making sure that all your contact information is visible in all pages of your website, you can also add a contact form. This way, you're giving your clients a way to contact you while they're browsing on your website. A contact form is a simple way to show your audience that you're keen on listening to what they have to say.

It's also very important to add links to your social media platforms. While it's very likely that they got to your website through, say, your Facebook page, it's important that you establish these connections in order to make the traffic much swifter and effective in every stage of the process—it's all about fluidity.

Set up a testimonial section

A lot of business websites are adding client testimonials to their website as a way to strengthen brand credibility. This can help you make the right impression, especially if your business is relatively new. Rather than publishing generic testimonials, offer your existing client base a discount or freebie for every testimonial they allow you to publish. Recommendations from clients are a good way to establish your authenticity online. It may also provide some insight into what you are doing right; there's a very good chance that a lot of different clients may like the same things about your brand and it's very important to be aware of these in order to strengthen them.

Include calls to action wherever possible

Don't forget to add your calls to action on your website. A call to action is a way to prompt a response from your website visitors. It tells them exactly what they need to do while they're visiting different parts of your website. If they're looking at your products page, the simplest call to action would be "Buy Now!" because that's what you would want them to do while on that page. Do you want them to sign up for your newsletter in exchange for an ebook that you're giving away? Use calls to action to let them know.

Optimize for mobile

No matter what type of website you ultimately decide on, you need to make sure that your business website is optimized for the mobile user. According to recent studies, more and more people are accessing the internet using their mobile devices so it's important that your website is also mobile friendly. Websites have the tendency to look different on screen and on mobile so failing to optimize your website can make it look unprofessional, or worse, drive away potential clients.

The work doesn't end at the launch of your website. You need to be ready to make necessary changes as your business grows. You'll have to adapt to search engines and constantly audit how your website is performing. And while this may all seem very intimidating, you only need to remember one thing: always put your clients' needs first. As long as you're constantly looking for ways to make their lives better, you won't have to worry about driving traffic to your company website.

CHAPTER 3

Content Marketing

The problem that most small businesses face is the lack of resources to create marketing campaigns. While it can be very expensive to launch a campaign the same way that big businesses do, you can create your own way with the right strategies. Sometimes you just need to get creative with it, which is a good thing, actually: the Romans used to say that difficult times created strong men and this is fundamentally true with your brand. The lack of monetary resources can allow you to strive higher, to do better, and this is something that is going to separate your brand from the rest of the competition—one of the key elements to be successful in an area as saturated as digital marketing.

There are many ways to drive traffic to your website. But if you want to build and grow a solid customer base, you need to have a content marketing strategy; you need to have a focus of where you are heading to with your content. Content marketing is great for small businesses because if done right, it can give you great results at minimal cost and provide that level of uniqueness that we all want.

So what exactly is content marketing? And what makes it different from traditional marketing?

Content marketing involves the creation and promotion of online content such as blogs, videos, images, and social media posts, with the goal of generating interest in a product or service or brand and in this way generates far more traffic on the platform where it is presented. These kinds of online content may not explicitly promote the product, service, or brand, but they're used to capture attention using relevant information. Content marketing is not about your products or services, but it's about your audience and their needs; it's about attracting so they develop a certain degree of interest in what you are offering.

Content marketing is great for small businesses because if done right, it can give you great results at minimal cost and provide that level of uniqueness that we all want.

Traditional marketing, on the other hand, is marketing as we all know it; it involves the creation of marketing materials that explicitly promote the product, service, or brand. Its purpose is to sell the product or service to the consumer. Traditional marketing methods focus on the features of the product, or the inclusions of the service, rather than the story behind it.

Let's say you're in the cake business and you're looking for ways to get more people to engage with your brand online. If you're going to take the traditional marketing route, you can print out flyers and business cards with your contact information, including your URL, and hand them out on the street. Sure, you might get a few calls, but do you think it's going to get you more traffic to your website?

If you're going to take the content marketing route, you can share photos of your cake designs, behind the scene videos of how you make your cakes, and top ten lists of the most expensive cakes in the world (your content doesn't necessarily need to be about cakes, but you get the idea). They may not explicitly promote your cake shop, but they're very effective in getting the attention of your target audience and once you have your target's attention, this is when your fantastic content is going to grab them and never let them go. By sharing high quality content that is relevant to your cake business, you're building your credibility as the cake expert to your potential clients and this is essential because, as a target audience, we are looking for a brand that provides that level of credibility that we all need from the content that we are searching for or the services/products that we need.

Content marketing puts you in front of your audience and makes it easier for you to earn their trust and loyalty. It helps you build relationships, and at the same time, get your brand message across.

Why do you need to have a strategy for content marketing?

Content marketing takes a lot of hard work and patience before you can see results so, needless to say, it's really not for everyone—patience is a virtue that can be built after a lot of effort and dedication. While it may seem like the "in" thing to do these days, you still need to have a strategy in place to make it work for your business.

It reminds you to prioritize your audience

As mentioned earlier, your main concern should be your target audience, and having a content marketing strategy is a good way to remind you to put them first. This way, you won't be tempted to create content just to promote yourself.

It's pretty healthy that you have confidence in the type of content that you offer, but between that and self-indulgence there is a thin line, so you have to be conscious that a high-quality strategy requires you to know the target audience's tastes, preferences, and perspectives in order to obtain far better results.

It keeps you focused

Many popular writers like Stephen King or Ray Bradbury have often pointed out the necessity of having editors and readers providing points of view for their drafts because it allows them to stay focused on the message they are trying to convey and not going down in the route of self-indulgence that we previously stated—this is something that you should always add to your own content marketing strategy.

One way to keep your audience engaged is to create and promote content that is relevant to your niche and you can only maintain that degree of relevance through a process of professionalism and dedication. By following a content strategy, it will be easier for you to brainstorm for content that is connected to your business. A few important elements to take into consideration are the following:

- Simplicity is the key; content should be able to be understood by people from different backgrounds, areas and social statuses.

- It's not only about providing content that might be helpful; it also needs to be interesting and fun to read–entertainment is a business and you have to use it to your own advantage.

- Like we said on other areas of this ebook, your content should maintain a certain thematic line; that way you are going to transmit a higher sense of coherence to the people that might be checking your website, social media platforms or through your email marketing campaigns (more on that later).

It organizes your workflow

Running marketing campaigns can be very tricky, especially if you are the only one handling this side of the business. Having a strategy in place will help organize your workflow since you will have to follow a systematic process to create and promote your content.

A successful strategy is all about organization and making sure that every step, every decision and every process that you go through has reasoning behind it, thus providing the kind of results that you are looking for and establishing a much more serious workflow within your own brand. A few useful tips for you in that particular aspect are:

- Always try keeping orders as clear and simple as possible for your working staff, if you have one. You are probably working with a wide variety of people from different backgrounds, so it is important that you keep things simple and understandable in order for you make to sure that the results are as helpful as you want.

- Create a schedule for each week. It is very important that you start the week knowing what you are going to do in the digital world, how are you going to do it and, even more important, why are you going to do it–these are questions that are going to define your weekly activity and that is something very important to take into account.

- Always keep your workflow updated with what is going on; having a routine is helpful, but it can grow stale after a certain time, so, as we always said, renewal plays a very big role in staying current and keeping yourself organized with everything that might be going on in every other aspect.

Organization is a key factor in everything we do in life and this is no different when it comes to creating a content strategy.

It helps you monitor results

The success of a strategy lies in its results. By having a content marketing strategy, it will be very simple for you to check the outcome of all your plans. You will not have to second guess if efforts are worth it.

Numbers play a big role in business and this is something we have been pretty adamant about, so it is not surprising that we invite you to keep track of all the statistics that might be of interest for your company from one angle or another; Google Analytics can be quite useful in that regard and you should not hesitate to use it– we are going to talk about it in one of the following chapters.

Content marketing is great for small businesses because if done right, it can give you great results at minimal cost and provide that level of uniqueness that we all want.

It acts as a pillar of your overall online marketing strategy

Without relevant content, it can be very difficult for you to get the attention of your target audience. Why? Because today's information-hungry generation are more interested to know how a specific cell phone model can make their lives better, than the price or features that it has. A solid content marketing strategy will not only help you connect with your audience, it will give you the leverage to convert more visits into sales.

Content is everything and it shapes the entire perception your target audience might have of you; your whole reputation relies on the type of content that you share and the way you share it. The internet is becoming more and more dynamic, always aspiring to provide many more instantaneous rewards for everybody, and your own brand needs to stand out from the rest of its competition–that is when a proper content strategy comes to the scene in order to create a much more singular focus.

How To Create A Marketing Strategy

Implementing a content marketing strategy is an effective way to bridge the gap between your business and your audience. So if you're going to create content, you need to create content that your audience can relate to. And having an effective content marketing strategy can make all the difference in the world.

So how do you make one? It's actually very simple.

Determine what your objectives are

First, you need to set your objectives. It's not enough to post content consistently, you need to know what kind of content to create. Setting clear objectives will help you produce quality content that really speaks to your audience. You need to have a purpose for your content, and a detailed action plan to execute it.

For example, if you want to use content marketing for brand awareness, then a good action plan would be to create and post branded infographics that your audience can share on their social media accounts.

Know your target market

We all know just how important it is to define your target market, especially in content marketing. How else will you be able to create quality content if you don't know who you're creating it for in the first place? Without a target market, it will be difficult for you to get results because your content has no clear direction.

To know the kind of content your target market cares about, try looking into their motivations and pain points. Try to study their buyer journey to know what kind of content they're likely to respond to. It will help if you can tailor fit your content to meet the needs of your audience who are in the awareness and consideration stages of the buyer journey. Using the persona sheets, you can think of content ideas that will ultimately bring them closer to the decision stage.

Set your content marketing conversion goals

The most creative content ideas would be useless if you're not developing content with conversion as your end goal. A conversion is an action that leads your customer to buy your product or sign up for your service. If the ultimate goal of your online marketing efforts is to convert prospects into paying customers, then every piece of content that you create and post should lead to a conversion.

So let's say you've just started your business and you're in that stage where you want to increase brand awareness and drive traffic to your website. Your goal then would be to produce informational blog posts and social media posts that would encourage your target market to visit your website. If you want to convert visitors to leads, you can engage them with opt-in email newsletters and special online offers like free ebooks or "first time shopper" discount codes.

Create a content calendar

Timing is everything in the world of business; the moment you do things can shift the paradigms to your favor and make everything much more helpful for you. In that regard, it's important that you develop a certain sense of when the best times are to make a decision or to post a certain type of content in order to maximize possible results.

At this point, you should already have a couple of content ideas to reach out to your target market. For your content to be effective, you need to know what to post at the right time. A content calendar is a working document that will help you stay on top of things so you will know what content to post on what platform for the month. This way, it will be easier for you to run multiple campaigns across different platforms because you have all your content ideas and plans in one place.

Starting a content calendar is fairly easy. All you need is a calendar spreadsheet and you can then start plotting your content ideas. The tricky part is having to constantly update it so make sure that you set aside time for it every day. A few helpful tips could be as follows:

- Do constant research on the topics that you handle. Your content might be based on an area that requires a lot of constant news and updates. For example, if you are providing content about football, it is very important that you stay updated with what is currently going on and deliver content that fits that particular moment in time.

- Always try to brainstorm ideas and discuss with your working staff. The possibility of discussing ideas with several other persons might make things much more helpful and fluid for you at the time of developing a calendar–after all, it's much more productive to count with several points of view rather than just one.

- Maintain a certain difference of time between each post; if you publish something at 9 am, then wait until 11 am or noon in order to post once again–give each post the possibility to "breathe" in order for it to get the attention it deserves and to be able to maintain a level of normality that you require.

Get inspiration for your content

For your content strategy to be a success, you need to produce shareable content so don't just stick to what you think you know and branch yourself out as a digital marketer. Do your research and check out what's currently making rounds on social media. Try to see what sort of content your target market is looking at or sharing and think of ways that you can put your own spin to it. You need to tap into their emotions to be able to create an effective content strategy and to do that you need:

- To check what your competition is currently doing; this is going to allow you to have a major understanding of what is hot in today's market and use what is useful to you in the foreseeable future.

- Check out new tendencies regarding your area of expertise; there may be new stuff that could be of your audience's interest and that is something you should keep an eye on–brand new events can lead to a new well of ideas for you to enjoy.

- Just good old fashioned brainstorming; just the mere action of talking to other people about ideas for your brand might help to get far better results in several aspects.

- Spend time out of work and try to do something that can distract you and keep your mind occupied somewhere else; it has been scientifically proven that overthinking does not tend to provide solutions for your problems or digital marketer's block, if you want to see it that way, so it is important that you take a bit of time off to do something else and that way feel much fresher to come up with ideas for your brand.

Of course, there are ideas and concepts that are generally far more appealing to some people than others and that is something worth taking into consideration when you are just starting out. It is human nature for people to want to help other people so it's no surprise that useful or helpful pieces of content generate the most shares on social media. Create blog posts, images, and videos that aim to answer your target market's questions or solve their most basic problems. Give your target audience a reason to share your branded content with their own followers; that way everything is going to be much easier–it's all about knowing what to offer and how to offer it; concepts that are different, but go hand in hand.

The most important thing that you need to remember about creating your own content strategy is that it should foster trust. You see, the more your target market trusts you, the more likely that they will buy from you. And the only way that you will be able to earn your target market's trust is by creating a content strategy that is focused on providing them with engaging information on a daily basis.

Trust sells. That is the most important lesson that you have to learn in this section of our book to take your content to the next level.

> **Trust sells. That is the most important lesson that you have to learn in this section of our book to take your content to the next level.**

What is considered engaging content marketing ideas?

There is no "one size fits all" approach to content marketing and we have to thank God it is that way. Why? Because it makes everything you do far more dynamic, challenging and it overall makes you a better marketer due to the several variables that you can find along the way. Just because some strategies worked for other businesses doesn't necessarily mean that it will work for your business; this is why it's important that you experiment with new ideas. Before you know it, you'll have a handful of great ideas that will become mainstays in your content strategy.

If you want to know what type of content has generally worked in the online marketing world, here are a few ideas that you can start experimenting with:

Funny / Lighthearted / Inspirational content

Content marketing is really all about psychology. When people are happy, they react positively. So if you offer them something that will make them happy, they will also react positively towards you. This is why it's usually the funny, lighthearted, and inspirational content that gets the most positive reactions.

Of course, the nature of your area of choice needs to be able to fit within this frame. If you are providing medical assistance or legal information, then a funny and lighthearted approach is not going to be the best fit for you, so you have to balance these two aspects until you decide what the best style is to get the best results.

Helpful content

No matter what business you're into, you need to remember that you're not just selling a product or a service, you're basically selling a lifestyle. The best way to do this is to create content that is geared towards making customers' lives easier and better. This is why blog posts are still very effective even after all these years.

One very intelligent aspect of creating helpful content is that you can share it on a wide variety of platforms and styles and still get a great reception and a high amount of traffic. Why? Because people are always looking for solutions for something; that is why most Google searches are based on doubts or questions that need to be solved.

You can share this content not only on your social media platforms. A blog, as we stated, is a very accessible and sensitive option, but it can also be shared through the use of YouTube, where the visual variable can come a long way for people who might need instructions to solve their issues.

This is definitely one of the best choices when it comes to content due to the high ratio of responses and reactions that you can get from your audience.

Thought leadership content

What exactly is thought leadership? It's when you establish yourself as an expert in your industry. People only want to buy from businesses that know what they are doing; that is why businessmen from all over the world are publishing books and becoming bestsellers at a stellar pace.

If you are going to go this route, it is very important that you are going to be capable of backing what you have to say and not trying to cover up your own lack of knowledge just because you want a bit of attention; they can easily spot if a business is only faking it, so don't try to be something that you are not. Instead, talk about what you do know and give information that only you can give. Make yourself indispensable by becoming an expert in a sector of your industry.

Remember: we are all unique in our certain ways; we all have experiences and perspectives that can shape the whole way we provide content and that is when and where you are going to excel, so don't neglect your own perspectives and past experiences because they can make one heck of a difference.

Rebranded content

If you already have old branded content that you think is still relevant to your target market today, give that a new look and add it to your content strategy. A lot of old and traditional brands have been be reinventing their already existing content, producing great results. One way that you take what you already have to the modern times is by taking new product photos to suit today's aesthetic.

Reinvention is a paramount factor to evolve as a brand; your old content is part of what made you what you are today and if it still maintains validity, then it is advisable to update it, adding something here and something there, thus achieving a much more complete product for your modern target audience.

How can you rebrand your old content? Read some of these tips:

- o Compare the old content with what you are currently offering. What are the differences? What are you doing now that you weren't doing back then and vice versa? What has to give? These are all questions that need to be answered in order to progress.

- o Is it still relevant? That is the main aspect to consider before even beginning to edit the content to update it for your modern target audience. If you don't find any kind of relevance for your current customers, then the best thing to do in this scenario is to discard it.

- o Change the terminology. You might have been a bit more uptight at the beginning of your adventures in the digital world; maybe you were still learning your chops and that is why you have to update it a bit so it can feel much more coherent with your current content.

Progress and change are inevitable, but we can never forget our roots. So when you decide to look back on what you have done, make sure to discard what is no longer useful and to keep what is still worthy and take it to the next level by using everything you have learned in all this time.

Customer-focus content

Customers love it when they are being acknowledged so try to think of ways where you can put your customers in the spotlight. Aside from answering questions that they send in through email in an organized and timely manner, you can also try delivering customer service through social media. Keep your target market engaged and happy by showing them that they matter to your business.

The best way is through live chats or making posts on social media platforms for people to have a chance to comment their doubts, questions and whatnot; interaction has come a long way on the internet and it plays a very big role in the way your brand is perceived–that is why you have to make sure that you are listening to what your audience has to say and can even learn a few things that could help make your brand grow while gaining your target audience's trust and even friendship.

Keep your target market engaged and happy by showing them that they matter to your business.

CHAPTER 4

Social Media Marketing

Here we are: the big, pivotal factor that is going to determine your whole brand's success or failure on the digital scale. We are of course talking about social media marketing and the high level of influence that it has to make you grow as a business beyond your own realms of imagination.

It's crucial for any business to be on social media. If you are not leveraging social media to attract attention to your business, then you are missing out on a lot of opportunities and falling behind the vast majority of your competition, who are already having a high-quality presence on social media platforms such as Facebook, Twitter, and many more. The great thing about using social media to get your brand out there is that it's cheap, effective, and puts you where all the action is without much problem. On social media, you don't have to go looking for your audience because most of the time, they come looking for you and they provide the kind of interaction that most brands are craving at the moment.

If you are just starting out with a small business, the pressure to accomplish so much on limited resources is always there. The great thing about using social media to get your brand out there is that almost everyone has access to it. You will be able to establish and build a brand at minimal cost. But what you will save on money, you will need to make up for in time and effort, especially if you only have a few people on your team. Here's a step by step guide on how you can make social media marketing work for your business.

Develop a great strategy

This is something you should have reasoned by now in this ebook: behind every successful small business there is a great strategy, and just like in other areas of online marketing, you need to have a great social media strategy. And how do you become great on social media? By being authentic to your audience and delivering the right brand messages according to your area of choice and the kind of target audience that you have in front of you.

Since you already know your target market at this point, you need to know what kind of marketing messages you want to tell them. How are you going to help them through your social media content and what social media channels do they prefer? Remember, each social media channel has its own list of pros and cons so make sure to choose your platform wisely. But more about that later.

Tie all your online marketing efforts together

It's all about connecting the dots, as the saying goes. You are not going to achieve much in the world of digital marketing by trying.

Treating each online marketing effort individually will only limit your results. So part of creating a social media marketing strategy should be finding ways to use your social media accounts to support your other online marketing efforts. How can you use your social media presence to drive more traffic to your blog? Or how can you develop branding with your social media accounts? How can you use your email subscriber list to grow your social media following? By tying all your efforts together, you'll have a higher chance of achieving your business goals.

A few ideas you might want to try...

- o When you post promotional content on your social media, always make it a point to include a link to your official website, thus making the connection much more evident and easier for your target audience to find said website.

- o Promote blog content on your social media accounts. Get creative and use Instagram stories or Facebook live to promote evergreen content on your website. The idea behind this is to promote interaction and a lot more reaction from your target audience, which is the main goal of social media platforms.

- Display social media buttons on your official website where people will be able to quickly spot them. This allows people to take a quick look into your most recent posts on social media and start following you as a result; it's all down to making connections, as we just said.
- Don't forget to also add share buttons on every blog post. After all, sharing is caring and we have to seize every space that we have in order to obtain much better results.
- Add a call to action to all of your blog posts and mailing list emails to follow you on twitter and Instagram or like you on Facebook.
- Integrate social media feeds on your website so visitors have a quick glimpse of the content that you're sharing. They're more likely to follow you if they like what they see.
- Your newsletters and blog posts should always be share-friendly. Add sharing buttons to your content.

Take baby steps

Developing your social media presence takes time so don't get discouraged if you feel your efforts are not going anywhere. Start with realistic goals and a manageable workload. If you are the only one working on your social media, choose one or two platforms and focus on those for the meantime. The key is consistency so include social media marketing into your everyday routine. Turn off your distractions and set aside a couple of hours daily to plan and execute your social media strategy.

The starting point is always the hardest part of any project and it's okay to feel doubts, but it's important that you don't allow this to bring you down; as we previously said, consistency is the key and with a lot of effort and dedication you are going to see the results on your social media presence that you were wanting all along.

Be useful to your community

The great thing about social media is that conversations are happening everywhere 24/7, which means the opportunities to listen in on your audience and be useful to others is limitless. Make social listening a habit as it's an effective way to understand your target market better. You will be able to monitor what people think of your brand, and at the same time, get inside information on what they really need. Just because you come across a negative comment or feedback doesn't mean that you should give up. Find ways to turn those negatives into positives. Take every opportunity to be useful to the community that you want to serve. If you only have the chance to create a good impression on social media, always choose to be helpful.

We all know that social media is about relating to others and maintaining a healthy communication with your audience. In that regard, there is much advice that we can provide for you:

- Always be polite. This may sound like a given, but not every brand follows this particular norm and they end up getting poor receptions from people; this is due to the fact that being polite, always answering in a proper way and always being willing to listen to what the public has to say goes a long way to establishing a healthy relationship with customers.

- Make an effort to resolve the issues customers might be having. One key element of being useful for our community is providing the kind of answers they might require to fix their problems. Perhaps someone bought a product of yours and they are not really sure how to use it; it's important that in this case when they contact you on social media platforms you can provide an answer and/or a solution to that problem.

- Be quick to answer. This is obvious advice: the quicker you answer customers' questions, the easier it is going to be for them to feel connected to your brand due to the level of attention that they are receiving–you always have to make sure that they feel valued by your brand's efforts on social media and on the internet as a whole.

Great communication and the treatment that you provide to your target audience is a fantastic way to be useful for your community. After all, no one is going to feel very comfortable close to people that don't value their efforts and that is something worth taking into consideration when you are managing social media marketing.

Create your daily social media calendar

Since running a small business can get busy really fast, having a social media calendar will help you stay on top of things. Every day, make a list of all the social media activities that you do plan to do for that day. Are you going to post links to your new blog entry on Facebook and LinkedIn? Are you thinking of posting motivational images on Instagram? Do you need a couple of hours to catch up on Twitter? With so much to do, a social media calendar can help you organize your workflow so that you don't miss out on anything.

> *Having a social media calendar will help you stay on top of things. Every day, make a list of all the social media activities that you do plan to do for that day.*

Invest in social advertising

Let's be blunt here: great businessmen know that in order to earn more money you have to invest, even if it is not a tremendous amount. Even on a limited budget, you can still boost your exposure on social media with social advertising. If you want to get results fast without breaking the bank, then you might want to explore social advertising. Paid advertising can help you get more audience engagement and website traffic which could lead to more sales in the long run. Depending on the goals you want to achieve, you can choose from different advertising solutions that different platforms are offering. So far, Facebook, Twitter, and Instagram are the most popular sites that offer advertising solutions.

Naturally, despite the fact that spending your own money is inevitable when you are running a business, there are a few precautions that you have to consider so you can never lose money:

- Create a reasonable budget. Of course, it's great that you want to inject some money into your efforts in digital marketing, but it's also equally important that you know how much money you plan to spend and why. Budgets always have to be reasonable so your finances can maintain certain stability.

- Make investments considering the kind of audience that you have in front of you. The reason behind this is that it gives your own investment the kind of focus and direction that you require to make it successful.

- As your business keeps growing, you can inject a little bit more money as time keeps progressing. The investment that you made at the beginning would probably not be enough for what you are doing today, so updating your investment is going to be necessary.

Never neglect nor reject the idea of investment because it is a necessary step to reach a higher level and branch out as a businessman or woman.

Stay consistent

This is probably the most critical and toughest step of them all – to maintain the drive to stay consistent on all your social media efforts. Posting content is just not enough, you also have to track, measure, and analyze the results. This is why it's important that you stay consistent in your efforts. It allows you to review your goals and metrics regularly. Once you've evaluated your progress, you'll be able to make the necessary changes to improve your overall performance.

Sounds like a lot of hard work, right? But it's also a lot of fun, especially when you start to see the advantages that small businesses have when it comes to social media marketing.

Here's what you need to know about social media marketing with small businesses: Small businesses have a better chance of succeeding than most big companies. Even with limited resources, small businesses have a better chance of fostering customer engagement than big companies.

But, why?

Well, first, small businesses are at that stage where they can take the community and individual approach. Small businesses need to rely heavily on the local communities for support so it gives them a better chance to foster connections with individual customers. You can still handle comments and messages from customers yourself so it's an opportunity to increase customer engagement.

Another advantage that small businesses can enjoy is that they can focus their advertising expenses on a small group of people as opposed to big companies and their nationwide campaigns. Advertising on the local level is not just cheaper, but it's also more effective because your approach is more personal. You'll be able to craft messages that your target market within your local community can relate to because there's that sense of affinity between you.

You can also collaborate with other small businesses to create campaigns that is community specific. You have the chance to work with other small businesses in the area to target people within the same niche. For example, you and another business can sponsor a giveaway and post it on all your major social media accounts. While winners get the chance to win prizes from both businesses, you and the other business can piggyback on each other's social media accounts to get twice the exposure. It's also a good opportunity to show camaraderie within your local community. As long as you're not working with a direct competitor, your efforts can produce great results for you and the small business that you're collaborating with.

CHAPTER 5

Social Media Platforms

One common mistake that small business owners make is taking on multiple social media platforms at once. While it may seem that establishing your presence on all social media networks is the fastest way to get exposure, it rarely works out that way. Growing your following alone will require maximum time and effort, and creating individual posts for every social media network you're on takes dedication. This is why, if you want to be successful at social media, you need to choose the right platforms that will help you ultimately reach your business goals.

Before you sign up for any social media network, here are three things that you first need to consider.

What kind of business are you running?

Is your business catering to consumers (B2C) or catering to other businesses (B2B), or both? If you're a B2C business, then you need to be where your customers are like Facebook, Instagram, and Twitter. If you're a B2B business, you need to have a professional profile and be where businesses gather like LinkedIn.

Where does your target audience hang out?

Aside from getting to know who your target market is, it's also important to know which social media platforms they're spending most of their time on. This is especially crucial if you're thinking of investing in social media ads since you don't want to be wasting your money on platforms where no one is going to buy from you.

What business goals do you want to achieve through social media?

Most small businesses have a hard time making social media work for them because in the busyness of it all, they completely forget about their business goals. Most owners think that as long as they post content (it doesn't matter what kind) everyday, that's already enough. It takes more than just a promotional post to convert visitors to buy, so before you start work on your social media marketing, make sure that the platform you choose has all the features and capabilities to help you achieve your business goals.

If you want to be successful at social media, you need to choose the right platforms that will help you ultimately reach your business goals.

Facebook

With over 1.37 billion people from all over the world logging onto Facebook daily, this platform works best for B2C businesses. If you can only afford to be on one platform, make sure to choose this one because local search engines now consider

Facebook presence to be a local SEO signal. This means search engines like Google put a bit of weight on Facebook business profiles when delivering search results. It doesn't matter if you decide to use Facebook as one of your marketing platforms, you need to have your brand on one of the most widely used platforms on earth.

Best content to post: Official updates from your company and your team. Behind the scenes of daily operations. Product photos or photos of your physical store or office. Special offers and events. Links to your blog.

Maximize your use of Facebook by:

- o Posting engaging photos and short videos that highlight your brand's personality regularly.

- o Making your brand seem more human by posting work photos that feature people from your team.

- o Running simple contests and giveaways that are specially targeted to your audience to grow your following.

- o Creating ads to promote new content on your blog.

- o Automating responses on messenger so that you can efficiently manage the influx of messages from potential clients.

Instagram

If your content is mostly visual and you have the resources to produce high quality images to promote your small business, then Instagram is the best social media platform for you. This photo app is popular with the millennial crowd so if your target audience is on the younger side, you should prioritize this platform. Since Instagram is also owned by Facebook, expect almost identical ad targeting features. It's great for promoting brand awareness and boosting engagement. If you're a local business, you can take advantage of the geotagging feature to make your mark in your local community. Instagram is also home to a lot of influencers so if you're into influencer marketing, this is a good place to start.

Best content to post: High quality product photos that are visually interesting. Photos from customers using your products. Behind the scenes short videos of your team at work. Photos and videos showing your company culture. Paid ads for company promos and offers.

Maximize your use of Instagram by:

- o Posting Instagram-worthy photos and videos of your products that are highly engaging.

- o Using Instagram stories to promote brand awareness. You can also use Instagram stories to show slice of life content of your small business.

- Running targeted ads to promote promos and offers for first-time customers. Make sure to use original high quality imagery because stock photos just won't cut it.

- Mentioning influencers in your relevant posts. Try collaborating with other brands for content on your Instagram page and theirs.

- Curating your Instagram feed so your brand profile has maximum visual appeal. Use a theme, color palette, or filter to make all your Instagram posts look cohesive.

Twitter

According to recent statistics, almost 74% of Twitter users say that they follow small businesses on Twitter to get product updates. If that's not enough reason for you to establish your brand on Twitter, how about its 336 million monthly users? Twitter is the center for all things news, trends, and even political rants in real time. It's also a great platform for delivering customer service because your customers won't need to call a 1-800 line just to get answers. It's the central hub where many consumers hang out, so whether you want to show off your products, expertise, or creativity, Twitter is the place to be.

Best content to post: Company updates (can be informational or quirky as long as it's less than 280 characters). Links to blog entries or links to content that is relevant to your industry. Retweets that are relevant to your business. Responses to inquiries posted by followers. Helpful tips.

Maximize your use of Twitter by:

- Fostering interaction. Always respond to tweets addressed to your account.

- Answering questions and giving helpful advice. Make it a habit to closely monitor your Twitter account for tagged tweets.

- Interacting with influencers who are already well-known in your niche or industry. Get your name out there by engaging in meaningful conversation with the people who matter.

- Keeping your tweets short and simple. But even with a limited number of allowed characters per tweet, always make sure that your tweets make sense. Don't spam!

- Using the right hash tags to join in on a trending topic. Use relevant hashtags on tweets that you would like your target audience to discover.

YouTube

If you have a lot of video content, or at least see the potential of promoting your small business using video content, then sign up with YouTube. This video sharing platform is home to almost 1.5 billion users per month, with most of them spending an hour or more watching videos on their mobile devices. This network is great for small businesses that sell specialty products that need instructional information. Unlike other social media networks, where you need to pay a fee upfront to get additional exposure, YouTube doesn't charge you any fees. As long as your content has the potential to go viral, it's up to the users to share it on their social media accounts. Choose YouTube if you want to increase your target audience through innovative video content.

Best content to post: Promotional videos for your products and services. Short quirky clips that show off your brand's personality. Animated clips of how-to or list articles from your blog. Behind the scenes, an intimate look into your company culture. Business events that you participated in or organized. Unboxing videos of your products by bloggers or influencers. Product reviews.

Maximize your use of YouTube by:

- o Posting video content regularly, even if it's just a short explainer video or a repurposed infographic. Tutorials also work wonders on YouTube.

- o Creating webinars and going live to your audience at least once a month. Develop a series of special webinars to cater to different segments of your target market.

- o Engaging with your audience. Reply to comments as soon as possible. Avoid copy-pasting your replies. Personalize each response.

- Customizing your channel with your brand images, color palette, and links. Strengthen your brand identity by including your logo and slogans to all your videos.
- Encouraging viewers to subscribe to your channel and give it a thumbs up. Casually mention it around the beginning of your video if you're doing a spiel or you can write it in the description box with links to all your other social media accounts.

LinkedIn

For those in the B2B industry, LinkedIn should be your main social media platform. Why? Because four out of five people on LinkedIn have the power to make business decisions for their organizations. And they're not only powerful, they're also richer. LinkedIn members have twice the buying power than the average person on any social media network. This platform is great for sharing your business expertise and insights to your audience. And with its numbers growing, you have access to a wide professional network just by joining industry specific groups. On this platform, knowledge is power. The more information you share, the higher your visibility will be in your professional sphere.

> *Four out of five people on LinkedIn have the power to make business decisions for their organizations. And they're not only powerful, they're also richer. LinkedIn members have twice the buying power than the average person on any social media network.*

Best content to post: Official status updates from your company and your team. Special offers and events. Links to thought leadership articles. Links to articles related to the industry you're a part of. Links to your own branded content like blog articles and YouTube videos.

Maximize your use of LinkedIn by:

- Writing and posting original long-form content. LinkedIn has its own blogging platform where you can write articles and insert images and videos. It's a good way to establish credibility and get exposure for your business.

- Giving credit where credit is due. Share information from industry experts and send them a message telling them how much you learned or were inspired from their work.

- Staying on top of what's happening in your industry. Use LinkedIn to curate articles and keep updated on industry news.

- Sharing links to top notch content that's posted on your website. This will help you establish your credibility within your circle.

- Joining industry-specific groups. Participate in discussions if you want to expand your network.

Pinterest

If you're running a lifestyle-related business (home decor, food, fashion, pets, DIY arts and crafts), then you might want to look into Pinterest. This platform is considered a paradise for people who like to plan. Just ask anyone planning a party or home renovation about their design pegs and it's likely they will show you a Pinterest board dedicated to the project. Pinterest works best for businesses that sell highly visual products or offer services that need visual planning. It's a great platform for small businesses especially because once a person pins a photo from your website, it gets shared on a curated board for all the world to see.

Best content to post: Curated boards featuring product pins following a specific theme. Pins (title images) to your blog posts. Pins (title images) to your original YouTube videos.

Maximize your use of Pinterest by:

- o Creating a business account rather than a personal account. This gives you access to analytics and Pinterest advertising.

- o Creating thematic boards before you start pinning. Make sure to write clear descriptions for your boards.

- o Finding and featuring great visuals. Create high quality imagery for your content if you want to feature your own blog articles on Pinterest.

- Engaging with other pins. Follow boards that are relevant to your own. Support your niche but avoid your direct competitors.

- Inviting people to get involved in your Pinterest network. Create thematic group boards where brand evangelists and even your own team can contribute their own pins.

Google+

On the surface, Google+ works just like any social media network out there. It gives you the opportunity to be part of a community and connect with potential customers. But unknown to most, Google+ can have a huge impact on SEO and traffic. Its Google My Business platform makes it easier for your website to appear in local search results. It makes your company visible on search and maps so potential customers can quickly find you. This added visibility gives your brand a better chance at organic rankings. As long as you optimize your Google My Business account for your specific target audience, your brand will be found.

Best content to post: Official updates from your company and your team. Product photos or photos of your physical store or office. Links to blog content. Special offers and events.

Maximize your use of Google+ by:

- Making sure that your Google+ is accessible to the public. Add the Google+ badge to your company website.

- Curating your network using circles. This will help you manage the different groups you're following.

- Using keyword searches to find pages, people, and posts that are relevant to your niche. This way, you can connect with the right people.

- Posting compelling branded content. Prioritize sharing high quality branded visual content like infographics, images, and videos.

- Using hash tags to find and organize content. It can also help you find discussions on Google+ that you can take part in.

No matter what social media platforms you decide to use later on, here's one thing that you need to remember. Always aim for quality over quantity. Posting irrelevant, low quality content, on any social media platform, will not get you the exposure you want. It will only hurt your brand. Just be authentic and be social. That's really all there is to it.

CHAPTER 6

SEO and SEM

People from all over the world use Google to learn new things, find answers to their questions, and yes, find products to buy. It's become second nature to anyone with an internet connection to go on Google and search for solutions to their problems. Whether it's an effective home cure for acne or the fastest way to get over a breakup, just search for it on Google, and in just a few seconds, you'll have pages and pages of results.

So you see, it doesn't matter what industry you're in, the fastest way that your target market will find you is by doing a search online. And when it comes to web search results, the best place to be at is on the first page, on the top of the list. Businesses who manage to get themselves on the top don't just get any traffic; they get quality traffic that actually converts into sales.

So how do you get yourself to that elusive #1 spot? It's actually a combination of different factors and hours of painstaking hard work. But just to give you a brief explanation, let's start off with SEO or Search Engine Optimization.

SEO is the method where you optimize your website so that it receives visitors from organic search results. You don't need to pay the search engine for your website to rank, but for it to rank, you need to hire specialists who will do the work for you. And the cost will depend on the competitiveness of the keywords you're trying to rank for.

When it comes to web search results, the best place to be at is on the first page, on the top of the list. Businesses who manage to get themselves on the top don't just get any traffic; they get quality traffic that actually converts into sales.

The main goal of SEO is to get visitors, who are already searching for your products and services, to your website.

By doing SEO, you're not only getting organic traffic, you're also building a more user-friendly and responsive website. You gain a competitive edge because you're making your website more accessible to your customers. All they have to do is search for relevant keywords and they'll be able to find you, even beyond your business hours.

SEM (Search Engine Marketing) on the other hand is the method where you try to get traffic to your website by buying sponsored or paid listings. Also known as PPC or Pay Per Click advertising, SEM aims to get you higher visibility in the fastest way possible. You just need to bid on the keywords you're aiming for, and depending on how competitive is, you can choose to pay for your listings by impressions or by clicks. An impression is each time you sponsored listing is shown on the Google network, while a click is when a user clicks at the ad and gets instantly redirected to your website.

SEM can help you get quality visitors to your website, without the tedious work and time investment that SEO requires.

Investing some of your marketing budget in SEM guarantees that your ads appear to your target market at the right time. It can quickly get you some targeted traffic, especially if you don't have the patience or the know-how for SEO. And while you'll be expected to spend some money before you start to see results, you can control your SEM expenses to make it fit any timeframe and budget.

On their own, SEO and SEM can produce great results for your small business. But using both at the same time can help you yield greater profit. Even though they're often presented as two very separate options, no one ever said you can't use SEO and SEM at the same time. After all, they share a common goal and that is to drive quality traffic to your website that will convert into leads.

If you want to build a strong online presence for your website, the trick is to find a way to balance them both. Who says you can't have the best of both worlds? Here's how to do it:

- Pull out data from your SEM campaigns and use that to convert organic visitors. How? By checking which ones converted on your SEM campaigns and adding them to your SEO strategy. After your SEM campaigns have ended, you'll be ranking for those keywords because you were smart enough to optimize your website.

- Use both SEO and SEM at the same time to increase your website's visibility on search engine pages for the hyper competitive keywords.

- Segregate keywords. Those that are too expensive for SEM, try to rank them using SEO, while keywords that have a better ROI, leave them to SEM.

- Use high performing ad copies as meta description on pages of your website.

- Test keywords using SEM before you optimize them. This way, you'll already know if they're worth the time and effort to optimize.

Doing SEO and SEM at the same time looks like a lot of work, but by utilizing both, you're already one step ahead of your competition. Why? Because most businesses will only choose one or the other.

Of course, you still need to see if using both will help you reach your business goals. You might find that SEO makes more sense if there's very little competition in your industry and you're already ranking for keywords even with little effort. But if you're launching a new website, then SEM can give you that extra push.

CHAPTER **7**

Google Analytics

Considering what you have read so far, there is a pretty good chance that you own a website and know a few things about analytics because these tools gives you some data that would be almost impossible to find any other way. This data is essential to increase the traffic in your website or improve your content because it allows you to know a lot of things about your target audience when they are visiting your website. A few things you can learn from analytics are the following:

- o Where your visitors come from.

- o How they get to your website.

- o The amount of time they stay on your website.

That is just the tip of the iceberg: you can find a lot more information that is basic to you in order to develop your digital project and, naturally, to develop all the previous strategies and areas that we have explained for you.

If you are someone who doesn't understand much about digital marketing, blogging, SEO or informatics in general, you probably are asking yourself why this information is that important and the answer is very simple: you need to know your audience in order to give them the right product. For example, you could be doing a great job with your online store and getting many visitors, but not getting the conversion rate that you require or desire, which could be the result of you not sending the message (or in this case, content) to the right consumers so you would be wasting efforts, time and even money just for not having an understanding of this data. By identifying your mistakes, you will create a plan that will lead you to a better content strategy in concordance with your goal that could be to get more new visitors, increase the traffic of your current visitors, or maybe both.

It is that detailed information that you can get from this tool that can even tell you from what type of device your visitor is checking your website from and you can also know the resolution in what he or she is viewing your site, which can let you know if you need a mobile version, for example. Another bit of data that

Google Analytics provides is the route that the visitor goes through on your website and that can help you to fix your menus.

Within the world of analytics, the most important and popular worldwide is Google Analytics, which is a free tool and is created and managed by Google (as you can imagine), capable of giving you a lot of information about your visitors and your site. Google Analytics uses a very friendly, graphical, and colorful interface that makes all these stats so much easier to understand through tables and figures that compile all the information that you require. Also, Google Analytics offers a large number of reports on different matters related to your site and some of them are the following:

- o **Audience reports:** It provides all the basic important information such as sessions (number of visits that your website gets), users (number of different visitors to your website), average session duration (how much time every user spent per session) and other similar details. The audience report includes a few subdivisions with other kinds of information: demographics (age or gender), interests (what your visitors consider interesting), geographic (where they are located and what language they speak), behavior (interaction with your content), technology (what browser your visitor uses) and mobile devices (from what devices your visitors come to your site). All this takes you to see the profile of the person who is coming to your website, allowing you to prepare the next step in your project.

- **Acquisition reports:** This is a compilation of information designed to let you know what kind of traffic your site has. People can reach a website from a search of any related topic in a web searcher, directly typing the domain of your site, from links on other websites, from a social media account, and many other ways. In general, all kinds of traffic are important and the best advice we can provide for you is to keep visitors from all of them. This report will help you to identify if a change is necessary in your digital marketing strategy.

- **Behavior reports:** Besides the general information about the behavior of your visitor that you get in the audience reports, Google Analytics has a section dedicated to this matter. The behavior reports tells you what pages from your website the visitor viewed, how much time he spent there, and when he left. This tells you what type of content is more attractive for your visitors and what pages you need to improve in order to keep visitors there longer.

- **Conversions reports:** We already mentioned it during this book and it's important to understand that a conversion is every time that you accomplish a goal that you previously set up for your website. Taking the example of the online store again, every time you get a sale is a conversion. In Google Analytics you set these goals and these reports let you know if you are heading in the right direction or if you, at some point, lost the way.

- **Real time reports:** As you can assume from the name, this is a report with all the general information at this moment which is very helpful to gauge the results in an immediate way from a campaign or something similar.

In conclusion, Google Analytics is the tool that will give you all the information you need to reach your goals in a short period of time with the least possible effort.

CHAPTER 8

A/B Testing

They say only God does it right the first time and that is a saying that could very well define what we do and what we have explained so far. Even if you follow the instructions and advice that we have provided for you in this ebook, there is a very good chance that you will make mistakes on the way there, but this chapter would let you know that even while making mistakes you can improve yourself.

In the world of informatics, the term A/B testing refers to developing and launching two different versions of the same element to measure their analytics, establishing a comparison between them and finally, finding out which one is the better option. A/B testing lets you know, for example, which title and description of a product gets more traffic or what website's layout receives a better reception from your visitors. As you can see, the use of this method could be very diverse, but the final goal for what is intended is the same: to identify those points that you need to improve in your website to reach the traffic you want. For example: you are not going to develop the best content strategy if you don't hurt your knees a bit, as the saying goes, so you have to develop tests and practice to improve and iron out the mistakes.

A/B testing offers security at the moment to make a change in any website or app because it brings to the table some real information based on the public's reactions before the change and finishes the guesses or the predictions which leads to a firm next stage in the project.

First of all, before starting an A/B test, it is necessary to identify where there could be an appropriate change based on what the metrics tell you. The next step is to establish a goal that will be the factor to define the comparison. The A/B test starts with the development of a second version (called variation) of an existing element (called control) which could be from the smallest detail in an app to a completely new design. Then, the second version is launched: half of your visitors or users will see the control and the other half the variation. The user's behavior is measured by an analytics tool which compiles all the data and it gives you the results based on the goal you set previously. Finally, with the information that you got from the experiment, you make the most appropriate decision.

Obviously, this could get more detailed by taking all the data compiled in different A/B tests and making some studies that lead you to a better understanding of your visitors' behavior, thus using it as the base of future changes or even projects. For this goal, the best practice is to make one A/B test at a time with a few minor changes to evaluate the real reaction of your visitors.

A/B testing has thousands of applications for a lot of different cases in the digital world, from a single aesthetic change in a subtitle to a 180 degree turn in a website, thus making those changes with the least risk possible based on genuine feedback from the users.

CHAPTER **9**

Email Marketing

For many businesses, email is still one of the most popular ways to get your message across. According to recent statistics, there are over 3.7 billion people across the world who use email regularly, with around 269 billion emails sent and received per day in 2017. Even with the popularity of social messaging apps, email still stands strong.

So it doesn't matter who your target market is, what they do, or where they live, they likely have an email account that they check multiple times every day. Now, just imagine what it means for your business if you could get into that space. You'll have direct access to your customers and better marketing opportunities, which could eventually lead to higher sales in the long run.

When it comes to web search results, the best place to be at is on the first page, on the top of the list. Businesses who manage to get themselves on the top don't just get any traffic; they get quality traffic that actually converts into sales.

Here's the ideal scenario. You send out your promotional email to your mailing list of 100,000 or more. If you can convert even just 5% of that, you'll have 5,000 people buying your products or signing up for your services. And you walk away a happy, rich, small business owner.

Sounds like a plan? Well, not exactly. First, you can't send out just any old email. Your emails should conform to certain standards and at the same time, put your brand in the best light. Second, you need to build a list of people who have explicitly allowed you to send them emails. Sending unsolicited emails will only get you tagged as spam and get you in trouble with the law.

If you're ready to dive into email marketing, here's a quick guide to get you started.

Know your email options

There are many different types of emails you can send, depending on what you want to achieve. Knowing your options ensures that you send out the right email for what's appropriate at that time. This way, you won't end up looking like an amateur or unprofessional to your mailing list. You'll learn later on just how difficult it is to develop a mailing list so you have to make the most out of this chance.

- **Newsletters:** the most popular email type. It's a great way to stay visible to your mailing list. Think of it as a digital magazine where you deliver relevant and interesting updates about your small business. It can include the latest information about your brand, company news, and even sales announcements. The key to effective newsletters is consistency, not just in quality content, but also scheduling. A weekly or a bi-monthly newsletter can be a good start.

- **Drip campaigns:** automated emails that get sent to your subscriber list. It's a great way to communicate with your customers and keep them engaged, especially those who just signed up to your list. You can have your email provider send out a welcome email to new subscribers, a nudge email to those who haven't bought anything from you yet, and even a thank you email to those who just purchased.

- **Product updates:** not many people like receiving this kind of email, but if you can find a way to make your product update emails interesting and highly engaging, it's a great way to keep your mailing list informed of what's new and upcoming in the business.

- **Dedicated emails:** these are emails that you need to send to a specific group in your email list. If you're hosting an event for example, you can send out a dedicated email to those attending. Add a personalized touch to these emails if you want your customers to feel like VIPs.

Sign up for an email service provider

Now that you have a better idea of the types of emails you can send out, the next thing that you need to do is sign up for an email service provider, or ESP. Your email service provider is the platform where you will create and send you emails. Most ESPs are built with functionalities to analyze your email campaigns so you'll have a better idea of what works and what doesn't.

There are a lot of service providers out there so choose one that is packed with great features at a price that you can afford. Here are a few of the more popular names that you might want to look into:

- **Mailchimp:** one of the most popular email services available online. What's great about Mailchimp is that you can integrate it with your other content management systems like WordPress, Shopify, Magento, and many others.

- **Constant contact**: a comprehensive email platform that can help you manage your list and campaigns. It has a huge library of different email templates that you can access so even if you don't have design expertise, you can create a professional looking email in just a few clicks.

- **Active campaign:** this has the easiest system for automated emails so you can easily plan, create, and schedule drip campaigns on this platform. You can also segment your mailing list into different groups, making it very simple to send out targeted emails.

- **Drip:** the best option for those who have e-commerce websites. This platform will help you stay on top of multiple drip campaigns that you're running at the same time. It's great for keeping your mailing list engaged. The more engaged your potential customers are, the more sales you can expect to come in.

Don't limit yourself to this list. There are a lot of options out there so feel free to try out ESPs that offer free trials.

Follow the rules

Email lists used to have a bad rep because people just couldn't take all the spam that was going around. But these days, thanks to the CAN-SPAM Act, people can now feel safe in their inboxes. So what does this mean for your small business? Basically, you can't send unsolicited emails to anyone anymore. You need to build your mailing list legally, so you should have a list building strategy.

The good thing about using an ESP is that they're built with tools that will help you stay compliant. They also offer learning resources that will teach you how to create engaging emails that convert.

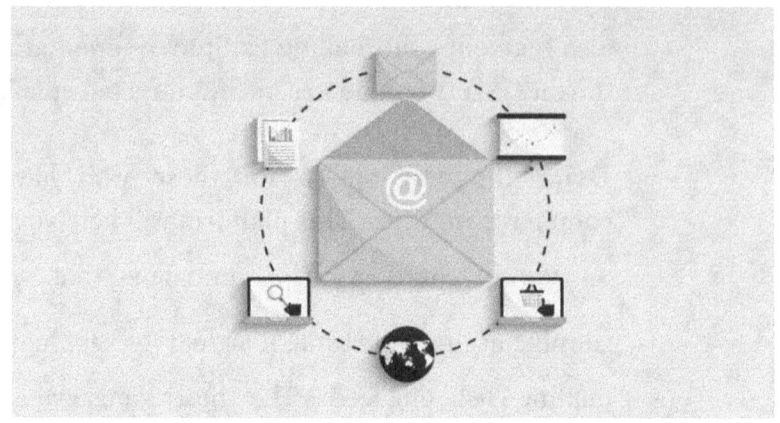

Build your mailing list

A mailing list is the lifeblood of your email marketing strategy. Without subscribers, there's no point of having email campaigns. Good thing there are many ways you can build your mailing list from scratch. If you still don't have one, here are a few tips to get you started.

- Install a sign-up form on your website and make sure that it's in a place that's hard to miss. Some ideas: above the fold, top right sidebar, at the bottom of your articles, the footer, or a pop-up. Aside from amazing and helpful content, try to sweeten the deal by offering your website visitors something of value in exchange for their subscription. A discount voucher or a free gift that they can pick up from your store perhaps?

- Make sure to keep your sign-up form as simple as you can. Try not to ask for too much information since people tend to get bored filling out longer forms. This could keep them from following through. Try to give your potential subscribers a "one click" experience to be on your list.

- Leverage your social media accounts to increase your number of email subscribers. Ask your followers to sign up on your list in exchange for something valuable.

- Set their expectations. Let people know what they can expect as part of your mailing list, details like how often you'll be sending them emails and what kind of information you'll be sending them. Be upfront about your intentions. It's also important that you put their mind at ease by letting them know that you won't be selling their information to third parties.

- Partner up with other small businesses and host a giveaway or event. This will put you in front of their audience and get some new subscribers out of it. Another trick is to do a newsletter swap.

CHAPTER **10**

Funnels

We have already discussed the use of Google Analytics and for good reason: they are one of the easiest ways to understand how to use statistics and analytics in the ways of digital marketing. So now it's time to take a look at what funnels are and what they represent for your brand's future in various aspects of their digital campaigns.

Contrary to what you might have thought, funnels are nothing more than the different stages a potential client goes through before buying your product or consuming your service. There is a whole procedure in their minds before they can make their final decision and that is why experts on the field have developed marketing funnels: a way to influence their decisions in that area to get far better results and accomplish your targets.

> *Contrary to what you might have thought, funnels are nothing more than the different stages a potential client goes through before buying your product or consuming your service.*

In the world of digital marketing, we are not always offering products or services; perhaps your brand is all about sharing content and you want to maximize your conversion rates– that is when the different stages of funnels appear and you have to use them to your own advantage.

Actually, Google Analytics offers funnels and they are one of its main attributes, so that is another factor to take into consideration when choosing their services in the first place.

The five stages.

All we have explained across this ebook plays a very interesting and fundamental role in everything we do with funnel marketing, but here we are going to present the five stages that you have accomplish in order to get the best outcome in this situation:

- o **First stage: awareness.** Obviously, you have to make an effort so that our target audience can realize your existence and that way start developing a sense of following for your brand. You can do that through ebooks, social media, videos, ads, and many other options that we have explained here.

- o **Second stage: interest.** Here you have to provide information and content that starts a certain interest from your target audience; they have to feel curious about what you offer and how you offer it in order to get to the following stage.

- o **Third stage: evaluation.** Here the client and/or follower is going to check and assess your content in order to conclude if it's of her or his interest. This is when your content has to be top notch, based around email marketing, digital campaigns, market studies, and a lot more–there has to be a reason for everything you have done to get the results that you desire.

- **Fourth stage: commitment.** This is when you show that you are the real deal. In the world of sales, it's a lot easier because you have to demonstrate how your products and/or services work so your potential client can have a lot more trust in what you offer. When it comes to content on the internet, it's a bit trickier, but you can show a consistent work rate and back your content with facts or statistics that might show the validity of your own brand.

- **Fifth stage: sale.** Or in our particular case, conversion. This is the final funnel and when the deal is closed; you got what you wanted and you can now start developing a long-lasting relationship with your follower by constantly producing quality content for his or her enjoyment.

It is not complicated once it is deconstructed the way we just did for you; these are all steps that minds, from the potential client's perspective, do without much issue and almost unconsciously, thus making the whole procedure much more natural for all the people involved. Therefore, it's important to have a few tips that can help you seize funnel marketing on a much better scale:

- You can develop all the aspects of your digital marketing strategy within those five frames; that way you are going to be able to maximize the results in every single stage and get a competent outcome.

- Install this mentality through your working staff, if you have one. Sometimes it can be perceived as an objective too hard to accomplish (becoming a notable presence on social media platforms), but through deconstructing that particular goal you can achieve a lot more and make things a lot simpler for everyone involved in this area.

- Use this for beta testing. The great thing about establishing these stages is the fact that it is going to lead to more high-quality beta testing, which is paramount to determine what strategies could work for the wide spectrum of an audience that you may have.

You are only going to progress through organization and through understanding; the better you understand how things work in your field of choice, the better your possibilities of success are going to be and that is something you should always strive for: to be the best and the finest that you could possibly be in everything you do.

CHAPTER 11

Marketing Challenges and Solutions

Let's come out and say it: it's not always sunshine and rainbows; sometimes we have to face struggles. You have a problem. Who doesn't? Every person out there is struggling with multiple problems. There are family problems, personal problems, relationship problems, financial problems, etc. And then there are business problems. Take comfort in knowing that you're not alone. The fact is, these problems are common to entrepreneurs.

Lead Generation

Challenge: You're not attracting enough new clients, not retaining clients, and you're losing sales.

Solution: Revisit your marketing strategy for reaching out to your audience. Are you doing enough online? Are you giving enough value to attract prospects? Are you pushing enough social proof that you're great at what you're doing? Are you keeping prospects and clients constantly engaged? Honestly answer these questions and then evaluate your entire marketing strategy and adjust as necessary. Introduce changes to your strategy and add a referral marketing plan.

Target Audience

Challenge: It happens; at times, you'll doubt if you're even reaching the right audience. You might also develop an inkling that you don't know who your target audience is.

Solution: Revisit your marketing plan or start again. Start with where you are and start small. Focus on a specific location. Afterwards, plot a demographic profile of your target audience. Consider factors like gender, age, financial background, lifestyle, likes, dislikes, etc. In doing so, you'll be able to visualize who they are.

Digital Marketing

Challenge: You're not sure if you're doing enough or if you're doing it right.

Solution: The good news is that there's no such thing as getting things right the first time in digital marketing. It's all about constantly changing the way you do things until you discover the right formula. As for you not doing enough, you can set evaluation metrics so that you can keep assessing your efforts against the results you are getting.

Increasing your ROI

Challenge: Despite all of your efforts, you are not generating enough sales.

Solution: Establish a set of metrics that allow you to identify and eliminate systems, processes, and strategies that are not working, and to keep track of your marketing performance and results. Focus on how many sales you have generated for each marketing campaign you have run. Innovate on the more successful strategy and ditch the rest.

Technology

Challenge: You don't know what kind of technology you need. What's worse, if you do happen to stumble upon a piece of tech that you can use but is not efficient and suitable for your needs.

Solution: Evaluate the processes that you have in place. Make notes of the possible processes that you can automate and those that need to be done manually. For the processes that can be automated, do your research by comparing and contrasting competitive software. As for your business infrastructure, you need a functional CRM, a collaborative workplace, an efficient messaging system, and a cloud-based platform to manage your intellectual properties.

Digital Assets Management

Challenge: There's so much going on and you just don't have time to go DIY on managing your website and other digital properties.

Solution: Outsource your needs. Tap on the freelancer market to have someone maintain your website. The same applies to your social media channels, content, email campaigns, and SEO. You can't be doing all of these things when you should be out there promoting your business in your community.

> *You can't be doing all of these things when you should be out there promoting your business in your community.*

Hiring Competitive Talent

Challenge: There's a huge market of top talent out there, but you just can't seem to find the person who fits the job.

Solution: Be clear about what you want that person to achieve and stay realistic. There's not one person who can do inbound, outbound, graphic design, website design, and website development, while managing your calendar and calling your prospects at the same time. Talent has a limit and it's more likely confined to a set of related skills.

In addition, be sensitive about what motivated applicants to seek for your job opening. What value can they get from you? Is it work-life balance? Is it flexibility of work hours? Is it growth within your company? These things influence applicant choices.

Establishing Credibility

Challenge: You can't find your place in your own industry.

Solution: To establish creativity, you need to create content, distribute that content, supplement that content with your Unique Value Proposition or UVP, offer something of value, and offer proof that your products or services are providing positive results. Offline, you need to position yourself as an expert in your field. Act like your brand tells you to: with authority.

Too Many Marketing Channels

Challenge: You're confused on where to market.

Solution: In reality, you can't be on every marketing channel there is. Instead, be where your target audience is and be good in it. This explains why some brands are only on Facebook and on Instagram. Others are only on LinkedIn or on Tumblr. Others only market on YouTube. And others focus on email marketing. You can be in only one marketing platform and be so good at it.

Time

Challenge: A lot of things need to be done in a day but you don't have enough time to do them.

Solution: There are platforms you can get into in order to accomplish routine tasks. Focus on high-level tasks and let these platforms do the rest for you. Of course, you'll need people to run these platforms so you need to learn how to effectively delegate.

A tip? On a piece of paper, write all of the tasks that you need to accomplish daily, weekly, monthly, quarterly, and annually. Cross out the tasks that you alone can do. These tasks should be high-level and revenue-generating. Afterwards, you'll be left with tasks that you can't do or simply don't have time to do. These are the tasks that you should automate and delegate.

Presence

Challenge: You exist but no one really knows that.

Solution: Create a marketing strategy that helps you build your presence online and offline. Focus on the core channels of marketing which are content, social media, email, search engine optimization, and referral marketing. Other marketing types such as affiliate marketing, paid ads, and inorganic search engine marketing can come later.

Stress and burnout

Challenge: You just feel tired. You feel as if all of your energy is being consumed by your marketing and nothing else.

Solution: Pay attention to your body. When you ought to stop doing something, stop. When you're stressed or burned out, you can't optimally function. The result? You might make mistakes and have to allot more time correcting them. So what you can do is to keep fit. Take a break from time to time. Your body is all you need to function. And yes, pay yourself so you can afford to take a vacation.

Conclusion

What's great about online marketing is that you don't need a huge marketing budget to get results. You just need to work smart and make it your #1 goal to engage your potential customers online. It's not the fancy design or the viral content that will get people buying from you. It's how you make them feel and the way you engage with them that counts.

Online marketing is an absolute necessity for small business because it has all the potential to attract customers, increase revenue, and strengthen brand presence. If you haven't started on your marketing campaign yet, what are you waiting for? Your competitors are already out there making their mark, so it's about time that you do the same.

We hope this book serves you well. We wish you the best of luck on all your business endeavors.

www.ingramcontent.com/pod-product-compliance
Lightning Source LLC
Chambersburg PA
CBHW071410220526
45469CB00004B/1233